TARGET ON GOLD

Goal Setting for Swimmers and Other Kinds of People

By Dr. Keith Bell

D0933402

Illustrations and cover design
by Karl Shefelman

Copyright © 1983
by Keith F. Bell, Ph.D.

Published and distributed by:
    Keel Publications
    3101 Mistyglen Circle
    Austin, Texas 78746

Library of Congress Catalog
Card Number: 83-80199

DEDICATION

For Bridger,
     whose goals all lie before him.

CONTENTS

INTRODUCTION

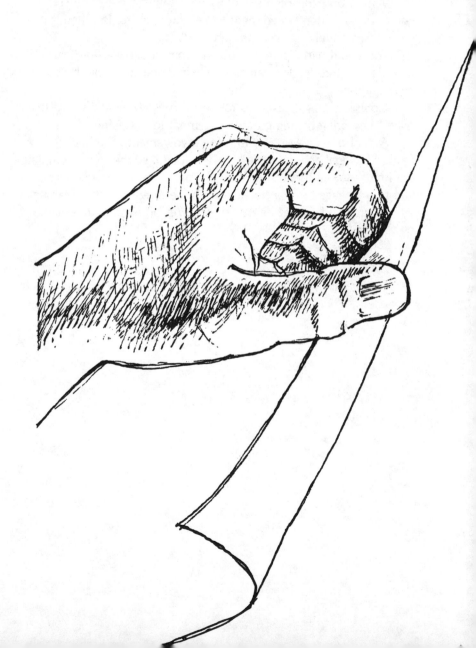

Filling The Void

Why a book devoted solely to goal setting? . . . Why set goals? . . . You don't need them to get through life. But then, . . . who wants merely to "get through life?"

You could participate without having any goals. But goals provide structure for the games you play. And they enrich your participation.

Goals are merely excuses for the games. They allow you to play. They bring meaning and excitement to the game of life.

A goal provides opportunity for involvement. The better formed the goal and the more highly valued it is, the more complete the immersion in its pursuit. A total absorption in the quest gets you truly engaged in life, feeling alive, performing better, reaping the rewards and squeezing out every drop of meaning life has to offer.

Why Swimming?

This book is about goal setting. It is written for anyone in any walk of life. I have chosen, however, to discuss goal setting utilizing some examples from the sport of competitive swimming.

Why swimming? . . . Swimming provides me with a medium for discussing goal setting in general and a form on which I can readily depict the details of goal setting in order to make fundamental ideas and principles more concrete. A further attraction is that competitive swimming provides the clearest of goals: victory. Moreover, the object of the sport is pure and simple: to swim a particular stroke across a specified distance faster than anyone else. And electronic measurement (to the hundredth or, in many cases, the thousandth of a second) leaves no doubt as to the results. Furthermore, competitive swimming is tightly contested at the highest level of excellence by such a large number of superlatively trained and thoroughly prepared athletes that it presents an ideal arena for the pursuit of excellence. All of which allows for the richest demonstration of, and highlights the importance of, careful formulation and utilization of high quality goals.

Besides, swimming is one of the things I know best. And I love it.

SETTING
YOUR SIGHTS

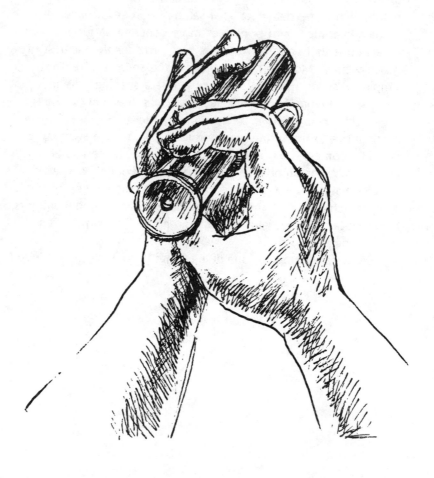

Focusing

Most often there is some reason behind how we choose to spend our time. Unfortunately, our purpose often gets lost in the shadow of our routine. Then, it's easy to get sidetracked.

Sometimes our actions seem purposeless. Our affairs get determined by circumstance, rather than by design.

In any case, it pays to acknowledge, discover, or create some purpose for your adventure, then to formulate a clear statement of that purpose. Such clarity helps you set priorities, make good choices, and stay on track.

The Pursuit Of Excellence

I have a strong bias toward valuing excellence. The pursuit of excellence seems to stand out as a purpose of choice. When conscientiously pursued, excellence engages as does no other pursuit.

The pursuit of excellence is a choice that necessitates high aspirations and concerted effort. As a result, action in the pursuit of excellence seems to fulfill many other purposes. In swimming, for example, pursuing excellence tends to be the best way to make it fun, fine tune your body, acquire skills, reap rewards, gain recognition, realize opportunities to travel, please parents and coaches, and fulfill many of the other purposes a swimmer might select. Through the pursuit of excellence these other purposes just seem to get fulfilled, often even better than when more narrowly pursued.

There are other ways to have fun, to take care of your body, to fill your time, and so on. But if you have chosen competitive swimming as the vehicle for achieving any of these purposes, they are best realized by doing it right: training and competing to win; striving for excellence and victory!!

A Word About Fun

Most often enjoyment comes as a byproduct of other pursuits. The fun comes out of being engaged in the quest. Part of your purpose, however, should be to have fun. No matter what you are seeking, it only makes sense to make the chase enjoyable. Moreover, if you remember to intentionally make it fun, you tend to keep a good perspective on your goals.

Why Swim?

The arena you select for your quest may be an arbitrary choice. The pursuit of any goal will serve to get you engaged in life. Any goal will do. You merely need to choose (and it is a choice) to commit yourself to the quest.

Swimming lends itself well to the pursuit of a wide variety of purposes: health, appearance, skill acquisition, feelings of self-efficacy, material rewards, recognition, team affiliation and general well-being among others. Swimming works extremely well to effect complete absorption in the pursuit of excellence because of the formidability of the challenges it presents, both physically and psychologically. It's an extremely healthful pursuit. And it can be tremendously enjoyable.

You might embrace one of these purposes, all of them, or some of many others. Just be certain you have a clear purpose in mind for your swimming.

Get With The Program

Success is aided not only by getting clear on your purpose(s), but by making sure you are aligned with the purpose of your program as well. Get a clear statement of the explicit purpose of the program within which you train. If your purpose is not consistent with the program, something has to change or conflicts will arise. Anyway, you'll want to know what the game is before deciding if you want to play.

Most swimming programs will have similarly designed purposes (namely: to provide an opportunity to pursue excellence in competitive swimming and to have fun in the process). Whatever the expressed purpose of the program, when swimmers, coaches and parents align themselves with the same purpose, the road to success becomes clearer, smoother, and more direct. Otherwise conflicts are imminent.

WINNING:
THE SWIMMER'S BULL'S-EYE

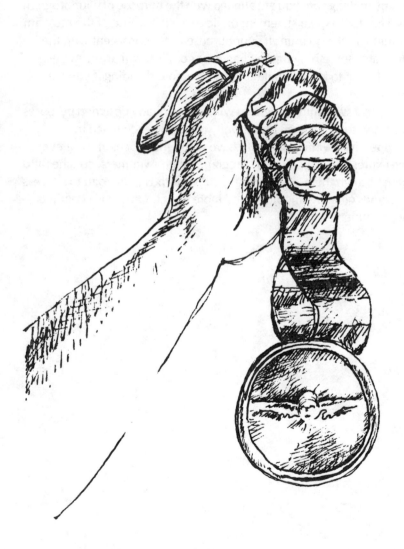

Pick A Winner

Swimming involves a series of decisions: deciding to do more and better; opting to shy away from the unknown; selecting goal-directed action; choosing to back off; deciding to go for it; picking the easy way; tackling the challenge. At every moment—your choice: whether you choose intentionally or by default and inattention. Why not pick a winner?

Opt For Action

Don't waste your time worrying about whether you have the traits of a winner. Determination, dedication, desire, commitment, and all those other so-called qualities that winners supposedly possess are simply decisions. Each of these so-called qualities reflects a choice to highly value certain goals (notably, excellence and victory) and to consistently display goal-directed action in pursuit of these goals. Who knows if you have these qualities? (Or what having them really means?) But you certainly can make these decisions.

Ability

Ability, . . . we all have it . . . sort of . . . maybe. But the ability to do what? . . . How well? . . . And is it causitive?

Can it be anything but limiting? Can we allow it to be confidence inspiring and open doors? Or, does it always come back to limit what we do? . . . And even what we try?

Easy

What's the attraction in "easy?" Training is hard. So what? What's wrong with "difficult?" See it as a challenge, not a burden.

There are very few things of value that come easily. Virtually all that's worthwhile is difficult to attain.

Comfort

How easy it would be, based on their words and actions, to guess that many swimmers have frequently put comfort as a high-priority goal. Complaints about cold, heat, and fatigue are far from rare. Easing up, or avoiding sustained effortful performance altogether, are commonplace. Yet, in swimming, comfort is not the goal.

It's okay to get uncomfortable. It's even okay to seek out experiences that are discomforting. Discomfort is not terrible. Often, it's growth producing.

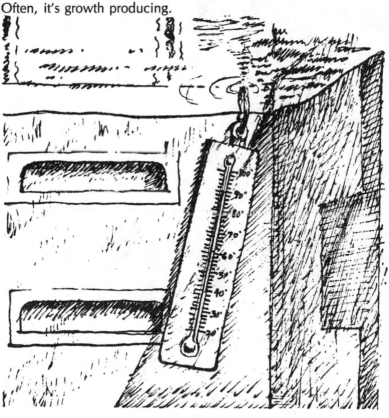

A Passing Thought

No matter how important it is to do things right (and training for competitive swimming surely requires that you do), doing the right thing is always more important than doing things right. I just thought I'd mention it.

The Forty Eight Second Yard

I could show anyone how to swim twenty five yards in twenty minutes and feel wiped-out from the swim. Obviously, that's not fast. Why would anyone want to do that?

The answer is: "No one would." It doesn't make any sense to train that way. True, if one put a lot of effort into even such an extraordinarily slow swim, one might gain some power and endurance. But, that kind of effort is unlikely to yield much in the way of performance gains when performance is measured in speed.

Yet, many swimmers train that way; and many coaches encourage them to do so. Oh, . . . not that slow. But often there is some goal-confusion. We learn that in order to swim fast we have to train hard and swim hard. Sometimes, however, we forget that doing so is a means to an end. We lose sight of the fact that the goal is to swim fast, not hard. Maximum effort doesn't necessarily yield maximum speed. Optimal effort does.

There is such a thing as trying too hard. And it is very easy to carelessly sacrifice technique (and, therefore, speed) in the quest to swim harder. Effort often leads to goal attainment, but the goal is rarely "effort."

Good Timing

The goal is to swim fast, not to swim hard. You shouldn't measure how well you are doing in training by how hard you are going. Certainly, the winner in meets is not selected by the amount of effort exerted.

Set goals to train at at least some specified pace. Then keep an eye on the clock as you train.

To know what times to select for training goals, set goals for those times you want to hit at the end of the season and in interim meets, designate desirable splits for those swims, then estimate a pace consistent with those splits for various training drills that will give you the best shot at reaching your goals for meets. To do this, you need to be familiar with pace charts and have a basis for knowing what would be good for the various drills you might swim in practice—all of them.

The Best You Can Be

"To be the best I can be" is not a measurable goal. Too bad. The sentiment is attractive. It sounds good. Certainly the intent is laudable. But, no matter how popular is such a goal, it's not a useful goal. It doesn't work. It doesn't help you design a plan for getting there. And you can't ever tell if you've become the best you can be.

The Goalkeeper

Peer pressure pushes toward mediocrity. It seldom encourages excellence.

Most of the time, people fail to value excellence. Instead, they seem to value getting by with the least amount of effort. At least we could assume as much based on their actions.

Most people don't set goals. When they do, they often fail to keep them in mind.

Others don't share your high aspirations. Neither do they respect yours or your right to vigorously pursue them.

You must fend off all the subtle, and not-so-subtle, attacks on your quest for excellence and victory. It's up to you to take care of your goals.

Winning

One might choose to participate in competitive swimming in order to fulfill a wide variety of purposes. The objective of any competitive swimming race, however, is to swim a particular stroke, across a specified distance, faster than anyone else. Clearly, the goal is to win.

Victory, and the competition faced in the quest for that goal, is integral to making swimming (and any other sport, for that matter) the rich and rewarding pursuit that it is. The quest for victory provides the best opportunity to excel.

If you hold the ideal of the pursuit of excellence as your purpose, winning is the goal of choice, as well as the object of the sport. As such, the pursuit of victory enhances the fulfillment of other purposes; whether they be fun, fitness, skill acquisition, weight control, physical appearance, whatever.

Don't discount winning. It is the goal. Value it!

Hedging Your Bets

While winning is clearly the object of the sport, victory is not something over which you have complete control. No matter how fast you swim, someone else might swim even faster.

Go for the gold, but also shoot for some additional measure of excellence. Getting beat while swimming an extremely fast time is not the same as winning the big one, (and shouldn't be celebrated as much), but it still has some value. Set supplementary goals that will allow you to feel pleased with that accomplishment.

Nonvictorious Victory

For that matter, winning is always the object of the sport, but not always enough. That depends on the competition.

Remember, you want to set goals that are consistent with purpose. If your purpose includes pursuing excellence, then an easy victory will not be consistent with purpose; unless you went fast or, in some other way, used the opportunity to better your chances of excelling in future swims.

Molding A Champion

Winning is clearly the goal—in meets. Preparing to win in meets is a major goal for practice. Winning is not the goal in practice. Swimming fast in practice, and practicing to beat others, is part of the preparation required to win at meets. But there are times when other things in practice need to take precedence. Sometimes in practice, for example, technique requires more attention than speed. As a result, you might have to slow down in practice in order to prepare for greater speed in meets. It may not be any fun to let others beat you in practice, but occasionally it may be a necessary investment in the future.

Illusory Success

Do you ever take shortcuts so that you will look as though you succeeded (leaving early, reporting a faster time than you actually swam, taking less than the full rest interval during broken swims, pulling on the lane lines, skipping laps, doing one-handed breaststroke turns, etc.)? Are you successful when you merely give the appearance of success? . . . Not in your preparation for meets.

Why do we strive so hard to look good, even when we are falling short? Who cares about appearances? It's performance that counts.

Make it okay for others to see that you failed, when you failed. (That's different than making it okay to fail.) If you don't have to look good all of the time, you are free to strive to prepare well all of the time.

Go for it. There are no shortcuts to success. It takes persistent, goal-directed action. And what we really seek is victory—not merely to look good. Appearance often only provides an illusion of success.

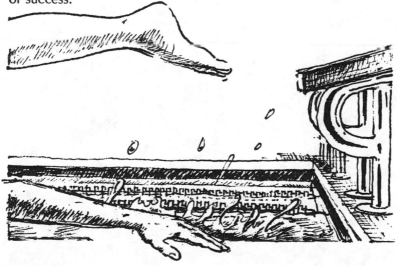

Winning At All Costs

If winning is such an important goal, doesn't that open us up to the dangers of a "winning at all costs" ethic (or lack of ethics!)? . . . Perhaps . . . but not necessarily.

Any goal can be distorted. Any opportunity can be abused. But the fact that some people lose perspective, forget purpose, and abuse their quest for some goal, doesn't diminish the value of that goal. It only points to the dangers of losing sight of purpose and distorting the quest. Winning isn't an ideal. It's a goal that best fulfills the pursuit of excellence. It shouldn't be put above purpose.

More On Winning At All Costs

In sport (and swimming is no exception), the goal of the sport (winning!) is merely an excuse for playing the game. The pursuit of the goal is what makes the game the rich, exciting experience that it is. To abuse the rules of the game, or the players, in order to win, is to miss the boat. It only provides for a hollow victory. Just one more case of the appearance of success without success at all

Fading In A Vacuum

Should the loser be consoled with the notion of personal best? . . . Perhaps. Certainly there are times when personal progress meets the requirements of success. But then, there are times when no progress meets the requirements of success. (Maintaining weight or fitness, and recreation often are cases in point.) It all depends on purpose.

There are many times, however, when your performance doesn't take place in a vacuum. Competitive sports represent clear examples. Personal bests might provide enough encouragement to keep you temporarily interested. Eventually, however, social comparisons become musts. Theoretically, you could improve forever. But if your competition also did so, only at a faster rate, you'd fall farther and farther behind.

Improvement has its value. But it's not all there is to it. Winning remains the goal. To strive to improve, without consideration to victory, puts you at risk of missing the richness of the experience.

TAKING AIM

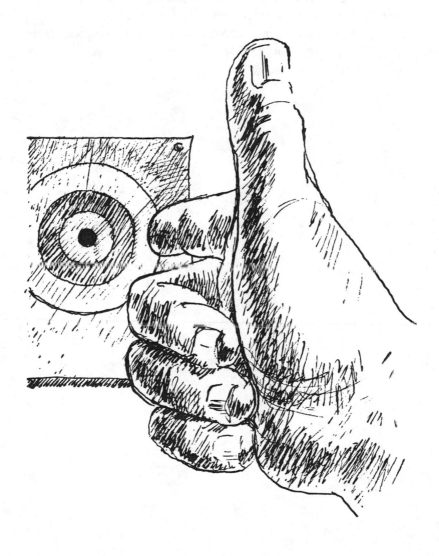

Zeroing In

Goals differ from purpose in that goals have clear end points, while purpose goes on indefinitely. Goals give you something specific to shoot for over a limited period of time.

Once you are clear as to a purpose, you can go about setting goals for fulfilling that purpose. Then you can devise an action plan for achieving your goals.

Brainstorming

Begin by deciding on some goals for your swimming career. These choices will be somewhat arbitrary. That doesn't matter. Just *keep your purpose in mind when selecting your goals.*

A good way to start is by writing as much as you can as fast as you can for three minutes on the subject of your goals for swimming. Uncensored brainstorming of this type usually works well to provide you with some heartfelt choices from which to make a practical selection of goals.

Future Goals

When formulating long-term goals, try to look ahead. What's good now, might not be good in the future. Certainly, times that were fast a few years ago are not that fast now.

Get out your crystal ball and look into the future. Apply some foresight. Try to get out ahead of the crowd.

Stepping Stones

A logical progression of seasonal goals should be identified. Identify the steps *necessary* for you to reach your goals and those steps *most likely* to reflect an adequate progression leading to success.

For example, making the Olympic Team may require placing in the top three at the Olympic Trials, but first you would need to make the finals. And before that, you would need to qualify to compete in the Trials.

As stepping stones you might want to consider a seasonal progression of goals, such as winning a state championship, making time standards for Jr. Nationals, achieving victory in Jr. Nationals, qualifying for Sr. Nationals, making the finals at Sr. Nationals, and winning Sr. Nationals. None of these are prerequisites for making the Olympic Team, nor are they sure-fire indicators of future success; but they make nice intermediary objectives that may reflect desired progress toward that goal.

A seasonal goal gives you something more immediate for which to shoot, something that is easier to feel confident about attaining. And such seasonal goals depict a likely path to success, complete with checkpoints for assessing progress.

Seasonal Planning

The period just prior to the beginning of each season is a convenient time to take stock of your goals and your progress, then to devise a season-long action plan based on your progress to date and your timetable for goal attainment.

If your progress during the previous season has fallen short of expectations; you need to change your goals, adjust your timetable, or improve your plan of action. If you have exceeded your expectations; you can raise your aspirations or speed up your timetable, while, of course, you remain free to decide to take even more concerted, on-the-money action.

Naturally, your season plan only will be a rough outline of what actions you want to emphasize at various stages in the season. Your specific course of action will depend on evolving opportunity and progress to date.

Ingredients For Success

Once you've selected your goals, you should ask yourself what it is going to take to achieve them. Identification of the ingredients for success will aid your plan of action.

Swimming fast will be essential to most any goal you select. The ingredients for fast swimming likely will include proper technique, power/strength, flexibility, endurance, speed, psychological skills, a supportive environment, pace/strategy, health, rest, and eligibility.

Building Blocks To Success

The most important goals you can set are the weekly and daily goals that reflect your immediate plan of action. The only opportunity you have to act is *now*.

Ask yourself what you can do this week to produce the ingredients for success (build strength, increase speed, gain stamina, etc.). Then formulate a specific plan of action that reflects the answer.

As with your seasonal planning, it's a good idea to write out your goals for the week as you approach each week; taking into account your progress to date. Sundays are often the logical time for such planning. List the things you are going to do in the upcoming week and set goals for their accomplishment.

Settle on three or fewer high-priority goals to focus on for the week. That way you can do them justice without feeling overwhelmed or overburdened.

Daily action toward goal-attainment will form the blocks that build a strong foundation for achieving success. Weekly goals will guide that action. Without a strong base made up of frequent, vigorous, goal-directed action, success can come toppling down.

Good Connections

Working backward, as described previously, from purpose, through long-term goals and intermediary goals, to an action plan, brings meaning to your daily activities. The process enables you to make the connection between each thing you are doing in your daily training and its contribution toward reaching your goals and fulfilling your purpose. Make this connection. It will give you added incentive to train and prepare well.

Potholes

Inattention erodes the consistency of goal-directed action, leaving gaps in the road to success. A purposeful approach to each task helps you solidly pave the road.

Strive to keep your actions goal-oriented. Get in the habit of asking Keith's Question and converting the answer to action.

Keith's Question: "What can I do to get the most out of this opportunity and have fun while doing it?"

Avoid Myopic Planning

At each stage of goal setting, you should check to see that your goals and your action plan conform to purpose. There's something to be said for being alert to the danger inherent in not seeing "the forest for the trees."

SHAPING
THE TARGET

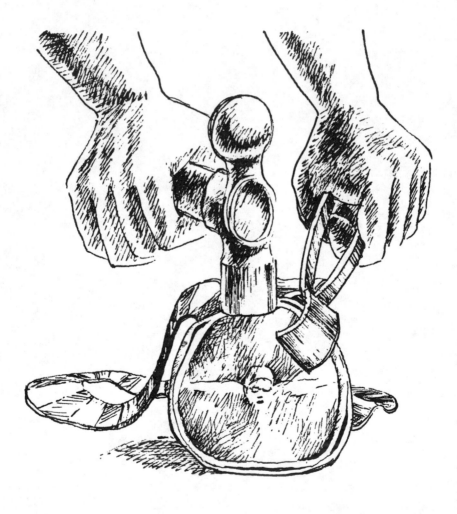

Pinpointing Action

In attempting to develop an action plan for reaching long-term goals, many swimmers come up with broad abstract statements of good intentions such as: to improve my attitude, get motivated, work harder, etc. However noble these statements, goals need to be more clearly specified. Goals work best when they reflect clearly specified behaviors to be performed.

Ask yourself what you can do to fulfill these intentions. "How would I know when my attitude has improved? What will I be *doing* differently?" "What would someone see me *doing* that he would know I was motivated?" "How hard am I working now? What can I *do* to train better?"

The Do Principle

Positive goals direct action. Negative goals draw attention to the very thing to be avoided. A swimmer can strive to attend at least nine of the eleven practices offered in a given week. But how would a swimmer go about not missing practice (other than by attending practice)?

Negative goals only describe what you don't want to do. They don't tell you what to do. Even worse, they get you imaginally practicing the wrong action as you go over and over it in your head. Fortunately, virtually any goal can be expressed positively, so that what you strive to do will automatically prevent what you wish to avoid.

Set positive goals. Goals should reflect desirable behavior you would like to increase. Goals to do something are much more easily attained than goals to not do something.

Yardsticks

Goals should be measurable. They should have distinct end points that can be assessed and compared to some set standard. How else can you assess your performance?

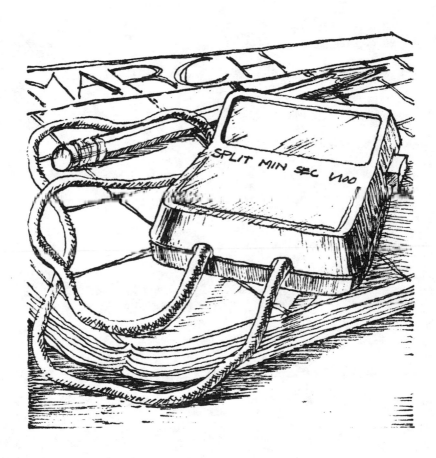

The Numbers Game

Goals work best when quantified. Attach numbers to your goals.

Round Numbers

Oh the curse of round numbers! . . . We use them and our goals become so common (e.g., to break a minute). We use them and improvement becomes so much more difficult. They sound so hard (e.g., to break a 20-second 50). We tend to try such large steps (e.g., we shoot for 1:10s and 1:05s, failing to discover and adapt to 1:07s and 1:06s). We tend to round off our results in their direction; in the process deceiving ourselves about our success (e.g., we hold a series of 100s at 1:07+ and kid ourselves into thinking we reached our goal of holding 1:07s).

Round numbers . . . so damaging. But they are so easy to select, and we are so used to choosing them!

The Phantom Dream

Goals work best when they are time-limited. Specify when you will complete your goals. Without doing so, you run the risks of procrastinating goal-directed action and making a goal ethereal: like a wish—or the phantom dream that is yearned for, but seldom chased down.

Goals Of Putty

Goals should be flexible. Remember they are your tools. Use them. Don't let them control you.

A good goal, like a good tool, is one that works. If it doesn't work, get a handle on one that fits. Remold it. Or use another tool.

Black And White

Goals should be written out. Putting them down on paper forces you to state your goals clearly. And written goals tend to elicit a greater commitment to action.

Out On A Limb

Goals should be made public. Write them out and post them for all to see. Tell others your goals. Make a point of talking about your goals.

Public goals solidify your commitment to action. They also contribute to a climate where teammates can better work together, mutually supporting each other and encouraging action for excellence.

The Flaw In Flawlessness

Perfection is not a perfect goal. It's not even a good one. Most of the time perfectionistic goals are unattainable. Even when they're not, you remain fallible. Omit the words "always" and "never" when you formulate your goals. They rarely contribute to good goals.

The Artistic Touch

Your temporal view is important when considering perfection. Striving for perfection is not so bad in those cases where you are likely to succeed often enough to maintain motivation and confidence, and not get discouraged. Perfectionistic goals, if handled well, may even encourage excellence. After the fact, it's another story. It does little good to expect perfection when assessing what you've already done.

Viewing perfection differently from different points in time takes a special feel. It's truly an art to set very high standards, even allowing perfectionistic goals their occasional value, in pursuit; while assessing your performances more leniently in retrospect. But that's what works the best.

THE
FIRING RANGE

The Three-dimensional Magnetic Bull's-eye

A goal is like a magnetic bull's-eye. It attracts your attention and directs your efforts toward that one focal point. That is one of the advantages of setting goals. Like shooting at a target, your performance level tends to cluster around the bull's-eye, rather than falling at random. (How tight a cluster depends on skill, preparation, motivation, etc.) Nevertheless, the drawing power of a goal can also limit performance.

The tendency is for your performance to fall at or near your goal, rarely significantly better. Rarely better, that is, unless you give your bull's-eye some depth by setting open-ended goals: goals to perform *at least* as well as some specified criterion (e.g., to swim *at least* as fast as :57.67 for the 100 breast). A bull's-eye with depth provides freedom for you to shoot beyond your goals.

How Far Should You Reach?

Unambitious goals can restrict progress, dampen motivation and interest, and keep you from competitive performances. Overambitious goals can diminish motivation, lessen interest and enjoyment, yield frustration, and even foster attrition.

A goal works best when it is challenging enough to encourage continued, concerted, goal-directed action, yet not so difficult as to seem out of reach. Finding the best standard for goals is an art, but one that can be approached methodically.

A good rule of thumb is to select intermediary and short-term goals that reflect a projected *rate of progress* that will allow you to reach your long-term goals and fulfill your purpose. Don't forget to keep your goals open-ended. You always want to be open to making great strides.

Compare your projected rate of progress to your recent rate of progress. If they are comparable, fine. If your current rate of improvement significantly exceeds your projected rate for reaching your goals, then you might consider setting your sights higher. If the rate of improvement needed to achieve your goals far exceeds your rate of improvement to date, you may want to consider lowering your sights or employing a plan of action that produces far better preparation than you have achieved to date . . . hopefully, the latter.

You Can't Reach Too High

The pursuit of excellence requires high aspirations. Shoot for the moon. It's the only way to keep your goals consistent with purpose.

Long-term goals should be unlimited. Unattainable goals can diminish interest and motivation, and promote attrition. But we can never truly know if goals are unattainable. We can only acknowledge when we've run out of time or opportunity. In the meantime, you want to open yourself up to the idea of swimming faster than you ever thought possible. As long as you have a reasonable amount of time to pursue your goals, you should be able to draw up a timetable that will give you a good shot. Your action plan should include goals for each week that are readily within reach if you exhibit concerted, applied action. Then, your efforts should be focused on these goals.

A good action plan, a reasonable timetable, two-tiered goals, a focus on immediate action, and an open mind free you up to unabashedly reach for the stars; opening the door to unlimited excellence.

The Best Of Both Worlds

Goals should challenge you and spur you on to concerted action. You shouldn't be satisfied with goals that fall easily within your reach. You want to strive for goals that are readily attainable with only the most persistent, conscientious, goal-directed action. You want to choose goals that will get you stretching your limits and reaching for the stars.

Yet, should you be discouraged if you don't reach the stars, but merely improve? I think not. If your best time is a :57.6 and you are shooting for at least a :55.7, should you get down about a :56.9? . . . No. A :56.9 is not what you were shooting for, but it's still an improvement. You want to be pleased with progress. That will help you stay on track.

Set two-tiered goals. Set a goal to go at least as fast as some time on which you are going to focus your training and meet efforts and a second goal with which you would be minimally pleased if you swam at least that fast. Put the second one aside, only to be considered in assessing your performance after the fact. But definitely put the second one aside! You don't want to have it around on which to fall back. If you have something to fall back on, you tend to fall back.

Look Beyond Your Goals

To date, only two men have ever won events in the U.S. Senior National Swimming Championships the first time they swam in the meet. Why? . . . Well, most notably is the fact that most swimmers set their goals to get there, to make qualifying standards. Then, when they do, their season is over. They celebrate and look forward to going to the meet—going there— with little thought to *swimming fast* in the meet. They usually have failed to set any goals for when they get there. As a result, most swimmers stink up the pool in their first national competition.

You have to look beyond your goals. Focus on and direct your efforts toward achieving a high-priority goal. But ask yourself what you are going to do when you get there. Don't end up falling short, because you failed to look ahead.

SCORING

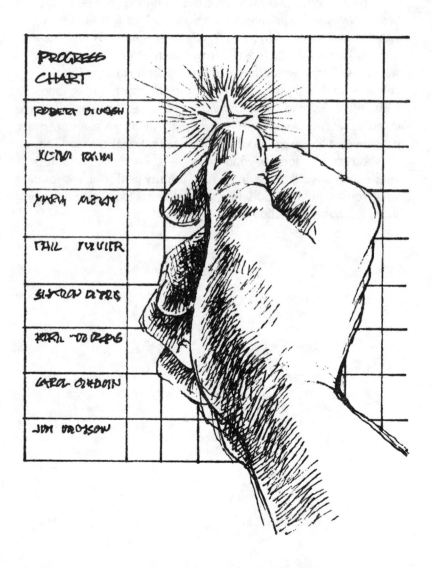

Score As You Go

Each week's goals should be based on an assessment of the previous week's performance. This will allow you to pause, reflect on purpose, enjoy any progress you have made, and make adjustments as necessary.

If you do not find it too burdensome, take a few moments at the end of the day (or immediately following practice) to assess that day's activities and review your plan for the next day. Even better, check once in a while to make sure the actions you have just completed are consistent with your goals and reflective of purpose. Just don't interrupt the flow by trying to assess how you are doing while you are doing it. And, keep it fun. Most importantly, do not mistakenly slide from evaluating your acts into judging your Self.

Don't Look Back

There's no value in dwelling on the results of past performances. After the fact, you have either succeeded in reaching your goal, or you have failed to do so. In either case, that opportunity is now over. It's time to get on to something new.

Well, Maybe An Occasional Peek Over The Shoulder

If you have succeeded—fine, celebrate. Then, set your sights on a new and more difficult challenge. An occasional glance back might provide some encouragement, confidence, and incentive for future action. Reliving excellent performances and their accompanying excitement can help you to better prepare for future challenges. But, don't allow yourself to be satisfied with your victory. Excellence is nurtured by success without satisfaction.

If you have failed, it is okay to feel briefly disappointed. But don't dwell on it. Instead, take *one* quick look at what you did, or failed to do, so that you might better readjust your goals or alter your plan of action. Then, get on to the challenges that lie ahead.

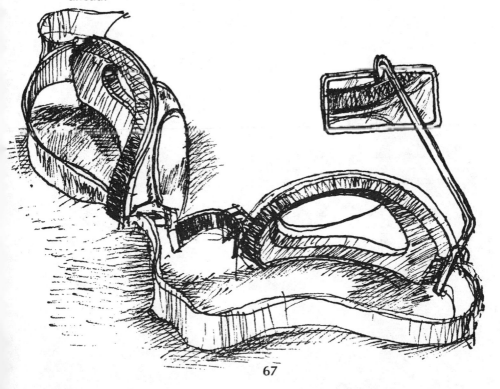

The Noncataclysmic Chasm

Failure reflects a gap between expectations and performance. That's all.

It makes sense to follow failure with adjustment. Change your goals. Rebuild your action plan. Or, improve your execution. The rewards for success are real. But failure, by no means, is the end of the world . . . or even a split in the Earth's surface.

Temporally-viewed Value

The proper temporal view of goals keeps everything in perspective, makes it fun, and aids performance. No one says you have to value your goals equally across time.

Goals serve to set up the chase. Total absorption in the quest for challenging goals brings meaning, excitement, and zest to existence. Therefore, it makes sense to highly value goals such as excellence and winning . . . *before the fact!* You are equally free, however, to attach little importance to your goals after the fact. Poor swims, losing, and failure do not have any dire consequences. They are unimportant. They're not worthy of your attention. Temporary slight disappointment may be appropriate. But that's all.

Likewise, winning doesn't matter that much either . . . *after the fact!* True, there are rewards for victory. That's nice and a cause for brief celebration. But that's all. Then, on to new challenges. All a goal does is change your circumstances; it doesn't change you. After the fact, winning and losing, and certainly who won or lost, just are not that big a deal.

Doing Your Best

What if you really tried, you gave it a superlative effort, and still didn't win? Is winning the only thing that is important, or does trying count? Isn't it enough to do the best you can?

The answer is not so simple. Only one person wins each event. If winning is the only measure of goal-attainment and success, then we have a very large number of people failing to reach their goals each time out. That creates problems. Failure can contribute to a decline in interest. It can diminish motivation. And it can bring into question one's capacity to compete effectively.

On the other hand, how would we know for sure if you really did your best? How could we ever possibly know what is the best you can do? For that matter, how do we measure whether or not you tried? Furthermore, there is a real world out there where the spoils really do go to the victor. Trying may be admirable, but it may teach us that it's okay to fall short in a world where, if you want to prosper or, sometimes, even to survive, falling short really isn't okay. As Winston Churchill once said, "Sometimes it's not enough to do the best you can. Sometimes you have to do what's required."

Try-learning

"Trying" refers to putting forth effort toward a specific end. Effort may be admirable, but not always functional. Thus, the "forty eight second yard."

To "try" is to make an attempt. What if your attempt was misdirected: you went about it in the wrong way? If failing is okay "as long as you tried," what have you learned? . . . Probably nothing about the right way . . . only that you are "okay" if you made an attempt, no matter how misdirected that attempt was. . . . What's so noble about that? Do you want to learn to try; or do you want to succeed?

Here Come Da Judge

Why is failure okay "as long as you tried?" It's not. It is not okay to fail. Failure is not the goal (except perhaps in physical conditioning where the body adapts to muscle failure and grows stronger—but that's another sense of failure). Failure doesn't get you anywhere.

I think this whole "as long as you tried" thing is rooted in our idiotic social and personal devotion to judging ourselves based on what we do. We get confused. We mistakenly equate failing with being a failure. Then, we need to reassure ourselves and each other that *we* are okay, even if we failed, by excusing ourselves because we "tried." It's best never to put your "okayness" at issue. Why judge your Self at all? It's not okay to fail. Failure has its problems—for you, and perhaps for others. But you are not a failure, if and when you fail.

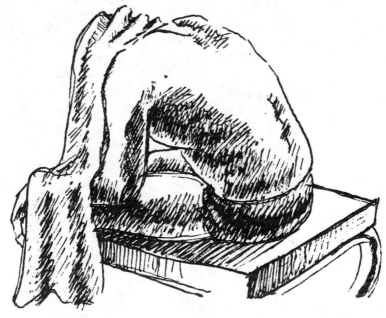

Cobblestone Intentions

We appease the judge by appealing to our intentions. Too often it seems that it's okay to fail (meaning we're okay when we fail) as long as we "meant well" and gave it a good effort.

But how do we assess whether our intent was good? . . . An ample dose of disappointment? . . . well-displayed public frustration? . . . self-criticism? . . . apology? What kinds of lessons are here? How do we learn from this? . . . And, . . . what was that about how the road to Hell is paved?!

Lurking In The Shadows

What if I don't reach my goals? . . . So what?

Goals are tools to help fulfill purpose. They are an excuse for the game. They help you get absorbed in what you are doing, enjoy it, learn from it, and feel alive. That's what goal setting is all about.

True, there are real rewards for goal attainment. And to miss the opportunity to reap those rewards might appropriately be mildly disappointing—but no more.

You only get depressed over not reaching your goals if you tell yourself:

1) it's terrible that you didn't reach your goals (when it's really not);

2) you should have reached your goals (when obviously you shouldn't have, because you did not); and/or

3) you are no good because you did not reach your goals.

Look out! Here comes the judge again . . . and you didn't even know he was there!

Personal

Swimming is a very personal thing. How well you do, what you shoot for, how you handle the challenges, the decisions you make, are all intimate issues.

Swimming involves extremely heartfelt decisions. You learn a lot about how you handle yourself. You expose yourself to terrific demands of what might be called courage, fortitude, commitment, etc. The decisions are tough. And it's very easy to take them personally. Judging your Self minute by minute based on accepting the challenges, making the difficult decisions, etc., or failing to do so, is almost inevitable. . . . Perhaps, that's what makes swimming so personal. And . . . perhaps, to avoid judging your Self is the most personal challenge of all.

Ensuring Victory

How can the sacrifices you make in the quest for your goals be worthwhile, if you fail to reach your goals? . . . What sacrifices? . . . You mean, the infinite options that you automatically forego everytime you choose how you will spend any given moment in time?

When you choose action in pursuit of your goals, you make *your best choice* based on the information you have at the moment (including your best prediction of the odds of reaching your goals, the value of your goals, and your estimate [with consideration to the odds] of whether the value of goal-attainment is worth the investment you make). Your choices are always based on incomplete information. And they are limited to imperfect options.

If you fail in your quest, it makes no sense to second guess those decisions based on the newly acquired information that you failed. You cannot go back and change the results anyway. Moreover, it makes little sense to spend time attending to items from an infinite list of things you didn't do, and therefore "sacrificed," everytime you do anything.

What does make sense is to correctly view your training as your choice of activities, rather than a series of sacrifices. Even better yet, take care to make the quest enjoyable and rewarding, independent of goal-attainment. Then you can't ever lose.

RELOADING

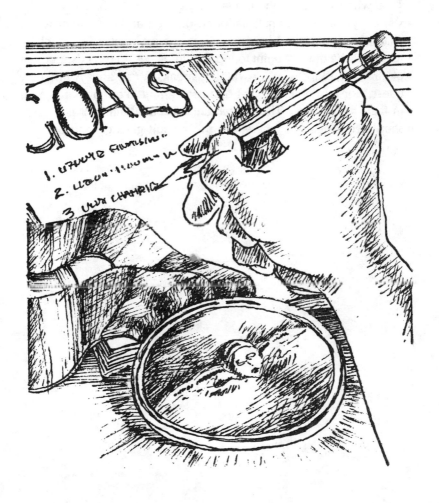

On And On

Goals clearly lend meaning, interest, and excitement to an activity. After we reach our goals, we tend to get lost unless we find other goals that allow us to reach higher. Even when it seems like there are no goals left for which to strive, we create new goals. Thus when we reach the pinnacle, we find new challenges. Winning a state, regional, national, or even an Olympic or world championship doesn't leave us without new heights for which to strive. We quickly point to top ten times, world records, number of championships won, or winning streaks. We'll always find new quests; for it is the chase that brings meaning to our activities and, in fact, to our lives. The excitement of goal-attainment is shortlived. The thrill inherent in the pursuit goes on and on.

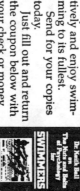
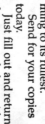